DATE DUE		

The Urbana Free Library

To renew: call 217-367-4057
or go to "*urbanafreelibrary.org*"
and select "Renew/Request Items"

CHECKERBOARD BIOGRAPHY LIBRARY

U.S. PRESIDENTS

The
United States Presidents

THEODORE ROOSEVELT

ABDO Publishing Company

Tamara L. Britton

visit us at
www.abdopublishing.com

Published by ABDO Publishing Company, 8000 West 78th Street, Edina, Minnesota 55439.
Copyright © 2009 by Abdo Consulting Group, Inc. International copyrights reserved in all
countries. No part of this book may be reproduced in any form without written permission from the
publisher. The Checkerboard Library™ is a trademark and logo of ABDO Publishing Company.

Printed in the United States.

Cover Photo: Alamy
Interior Photos: AP Images pp. 9, 11, 19; Corbis pp. 12, 14, 15, 17, 21, 23, 24, 28, 29;
    Getty Images pp. 5, 27; iStockphoto pp. 26, 32; Library of Congress pp. 11, 13;
    National Archives p. 17

Editor: BreAnn Rumsch
Art Direction & Cover Design: Neil Klinepier
Interior Design: Jaime Martens

Library of Congress Cataloging-in-Publication Data

Britton, Tamara L., 1963-
  Theodore Roosevelt / Tamara L. Britton.
      p. cm. -- (United States presidents)
  Includes index.
  ISBN 978-1-60453-473-3
  1. Roosevelt, Theodore, 1858-1919--Juvenile literature. 2. Presidents--United States--Biography--
Juvenile literature. I. Title.

  E757.B857 2009
  973.91'1092--dc22
  [B]
                        2008042046

CONTENTS

THEODORE ROOSEVELT

Theodore Roosevelt became the twenty-sixth U.S. president on September 14, 1901. Roosevelt worked to end **corruption** in government and business. And, he worked to make life better for working people.

Roosevelt had many opportunities to pursue these goals. He served in the New York State Assembly. Later, he was in charge of the U.S. **Civil Service** Commission. Roosevelt also served as head of the New York City Police Department. And in 1898, he was elected governor of New York.

In addition to helping people, Roosevelt wanted to protect America's land. He passed laws to preserve millions of acres of parkland. He declared several national parks and monuments. And, Roosevelt created the U.S. Forest Service.

Roosevelt also worked for peace abroad. He fought for Cuba's independence from Spain in the **Spanish-American War**. He also won a **Nobel Peace Prize** for helping to end the **Russo-Japanese War**. Roosevelt's accomplishments improved the lives of millions of people all over the world.

Theodore Roosevelt

TIMELINE

1858 - Theodore Roosevelt was born on October 27 in New York City, New York.

1880 - Roosevelt graduated from Harvard University; on October 27, he married Alice Hathaway Lee.

1881 - Roosevelt was elected to the New York State Assembly.

1884 - Alice Roosevelt died on February 14; Roosevelt went to Dakota Territory.

1886 - Roosevelt married Edith Kermit Carow on December 2.

1889 - President Benjamin Harrison appointed Roosevelt to head the U.S. Civil Service Commission.

1895 - Roosevelt became head of the New York City Police Department.

1897 - President William McKinley appointed Roosevelt assistant secretary of the navy.

1898 - The USS *Maine* exploded on February 15; the United States declared war against Spain on April 25; the Rough Riders fought in the Battle of San Juan Hill; the Treaty of Paris was signed on December 10, ending the Spanish-American War; Roosevelt was elected governor of New York.

1900 - Roosevelt was elected vice president under McKinley.

1901 - President McKinley died on September 14, and Roosevelt became president.

1904 - On November 8, Roosevelt was elected president.

1906 - Roosevelt won the Nobel Peace Prize; Roosevelt signed the Antiquities Act, the Pure Food and Drug Act, and the Meat Inspection Act.

1909 - On March 4, William Taft became president; Roosevelt left the White House.

1912 - Roosevelt ran for president for the Progressive Party but lost the election.

1919 - Theodore Roosevelt died on January 6 at Sagamore Hill.

DID YOU KNOW?

President Theodore Roosevelt was the first American to win a Nobel Prize.

Roosevelt was the first president to travel abroad while in office. He visited the Panama Canal in 1906.

In 1902, Roosevelt went hunting in Mississippi. While there, he refused to shoot a bear. A cartoon showing the incident inspired shop owner Morris Michtom. He made a bear stuffed animal. President Roosevelt gave Michtom permission to name the stuffed bear after him. This is how teddy bears got their name.

President Roosevelt gave the White House its name. Previously, it was called the Executive Mansion.

EARLY YEARS

Theodore Roosevelt was born on October 27, 1858, in New York City, New York. His father, Theodore Sr., was a wealthy businessman. His mother, Martha Bulloch, took care of their home. Theodore had an older sister named Anna. He also had a younger sister, Corinne, and a younger brother, Elliott.

As a child, Theodore was often sick with **asthma**. Sometimes he couldn't breathe. His family was afraid he might die. Some nights, Theodore's father would drive Theodore around town in his carriage. Theodore Sr. hoped the cool air would help his son breathe.

Because of his poor health, Theodore was educated at home. He especially enjoyed **natural history**. Theodore collected insects, mice, snakes, and other animals. He kept their bodies in his room and wrote down everything about them. Theodore called his collection the Roosevelt Museum of Natural History.

FAST FACTS

BORN - October 27, 1858
WIVES - Alice Hathaway Lee (1861–1884)
Edith Kermit Carow (1861–1948)
CHILDREN - 6
POLITICAL PARTY - Republican
AGE AT INAUGURATION - 42
YEARS SERVED - 1901–1909
VICE PRESIDENT - Charles Fairbanks
DIED - January 6, 1919, age 60

8

Despite the work of many doctors, Theodore's **asthma** did not improve. He was also small and not very muscular.

When he was 12 years old, Theodore's father challenged him to strengthen his body. So, Theodore learned to box. He also lifted weights, hiked, and swam. Slowly, Theodore grew stronger. And, his asthma improved.

As a child, Theodore was called "Teedie."

In 1873, Theodore began studying so he could attend Harvard University. His knowledge of science and history was vast. But, he needed work in mathematics. So, his father hired a **tutor** to help him.

COLLEGE MAN

Theodore passed his college entrance examinations. In fall 1876, he entered Harvard in Cambridge, Massachusetts. Theodore enjoyed his classes. He asked many questions in class and started lively discussions.

Outside the classroom, Theodore still studied **natural history**. He had hundreds of animals in his collection. He also continued his exercise routine. Theodore liked to row, dance, swim, high-jump, and run. In addition, he joined Harvard's boxing team.

Theodore was very energetic. He also loved to talk. He told jokes at parties and made people laugh. He soon became popular with other students.

In 1878, Theodore Sr. died. For a long time, Theodore was very sad. He decided to work hard and be someone important to honor his father. Not long after, he wrote *Naval History of the War of 1812*. Theodore would write many more books in his life.

At Harvard, Theodore met a young woman named Alice Hathaway Lee. He wanted to marry Alice, but she was not sure. Theodore did not give up! He worked hard to convince her to marry him.

At Harvard, Theodore became a member of the Porcellian Club. This influential social club was very selective about its membership.

Alice was called "Sunshine" by her family and friends.

In 1880, Theodore graduated from Harvard. That same year, Alice finally agreed to be his wife. They married on October 27, Theodore's twenty-second birthday.

Later that year, Theodore entered Columbia University School of Law in New York City, New York. There, he began to question the power that corporations had over workers and consumers. Soon, he would work in politics to change those things.

ASSEMBLYMAN

In November 1881, Roosevelt was elected to the New York State Assembly. At first, some assemblymen made fun of his fancy clothes. They also mocked his upper-class accent. But, Roosevelt soon earned respect for his work against **corruption**. Roosevelt was reelected to the assembly in 1882 and 1883.

On February 12, 1884, the Roosevelts welcomed a baby girl. But two days later, Alice Roosevelt died from kidney disease. Roosevelt's mother died that same day.

Roosevelt was devastated. When his term in the assembly ended, he left New York for Dakota Territory. Roosevelt's sister Anna took care of his daughter. He had named her Alice Lee.

In Dakota Territory, Roosevelt started two ranches on the Little Missouri River. They were the Maltese Cross Ranch and the Elkhorn Ranch. Roosevelt enjoyed working as a rancher. He raised cattle. And he hunted birds, rabbits, and grizzly bears.

Alice Lee grew up to be quite mischievous. Her father once said, "I can run the country or I can control Alice. I cannot possibly do both."

While working as a rancher, Roosevelt helped the sheriff chase outlaws!

FAMILY MAN

Roosevelt's time in Dakota Territory helped heal his grief. In 1885, he returned to New York. There, he built a new home on Oyster Bay on Long Island. Roosevelt named it Sagamore Hill.

The Roosevelts lived at Sagamore Hill until Edith's death in 1948. In 1963, it became a national historic site.

In 1886, Roosevelt ran for mayor of New York. But, he lost the election. On December 2, Roosevelt married his childhood friend Edith Kermit Carow. In spring 1887, the Roosevelts and young Alice Lee moved into Sagamore Hill.

The Roosevelts had five children. They were Theodore Jr., Kermit, Ethel, Archibald, and Quentin.

Roosevelt loved to play with his children. He filled the house with toys. He also liked to tell them stories. Sagamore Hill was a happy, loving home for all who lived there.

Left to right: *Quentin, Mr. Roosevelt, Theodore Jr.*
Archibald, Alice Lee, Kermit, Mrs. Roosevelt, and Ethel

THE REFORMER

For two years, Roosevelt lived at Sagamore Hill. He wrote books and spent time with his family. He hiked in the woods, fished, and hunted. In 1889, he was once again called to public service. That year, President Benjamin Harrison appointed Roosevelt to head the U.S. **Civil Service** Commission. In this position, Roosevelt continued to work to end **corruption**.

Roosevelt was against the **spoils system**. So, he made more civil service jobs subject to passing an examination. He revised some of the tests and punished those who tried to cheat. Roosevelt also made women equal to men in some jobs.

In 1895, Roosevelt was asked to head the New York City Police Department. Once again, he worked to end corruption. He disguised himself and watched police officers do their work. Those who did not perform well lost their jobs. Roosevelt even fired the chief of police!

Roosevelt wanted **Republican** William McKinley to be the
next president of the United States. In summer 1896, he worked on
McKinley's campaign. McKinley won the election. In 1897, he
made Roosevelt assistant **secretary of the navy**.

President McKinley (left) *and Roosevelt*

Naval Affairs   134

To the
Senate of the United States:

I nominate Theodore Roosevelt
of New York to be Assistant
Secretary of the Navy, vice
William McAdoo, resigned.

William McKinley

Executive Mansion,
April 6, 1897.

*President
McKinley's
nomination of
Roosevelt as
assistant secretary
of the navy*

A ROUGH RIDER

Roosevelt was excited about his new job. He liked battles and ships. And, he knew much about the naval field. His book, *Naval History of the War of 1812*, had become well respected.

During this time, Cuba was working to gain its independence from Spain. Roosevelt wanted to help the Cubans. So, he waited until **Secretary of the Navy** John D. Long was out of town. Then, Roosevelt ordered American ships to prepare for war.

On February 15, 1898, the USS *Maine* was in the harbor at Havana, Cuba. The ship exploded, and 266 lives were lost. Many Americans blamed Spain for the disaster. On April 25, the United States declared war against Spain. The **Spanish-American War** had begun.

Roosevelt quit his job in May to join the war effort. He trained the First Volunteer U.S. Cavalry to fight in Cuba. The men were called the Rough Riders. On July 1, the Rough Riders participated in the Battle of San Juan Hill. They charged up Kettle Hill and won an important battle.

The cause of the USS Maine *explosion has never been determined.*

The United States won the war. The Treaty of Paris was signed on December 10, 1898. When Roosevelt came home, Americans welcomed him as a hero!

FROM GOVERNOR TO PRESIDENT

In fall 1898, Roosevelt was elected governor of New York. He worked hard to make life better for working people. He limited the number of hours that children could work. He also gave state workers an eight-hour workday.

In addition, Roosevelt outlawed racial **discrimination** in public schools. He paid teachers more money. He also made laws that forced big companies to pay their share of taxes.

In 1900, President McKinley ran for reelection. Roosevelt was chosen as his **running mate**. The **Democrats** chose former congressman William Jennings Bryan as their candidate. His running mate was former vice president Adlai E. Stevenson. McKinley and Roosevelt won the election.

But only six months later, President McKinley was shot by an **assassin** on September 6, 1901. He died on September 14. Roosevelt was **inaugurated** that same day. At just 42 years old, Roosevelt became the youngest president in American history.

In the early 1900s, many children worked to help support their families. They worked long hours and did not have time for school or play. There were no federal laws to govern child labor. So, individual states passed their own child labor laws.

PRESIDENT ROOSEVELT

As president, Roosevelt worked to regulate big corporations. Many had organized into **trusts**. Roosevelt filed **lawsuits** to break up the trusts. The largest was a railroad trust called the Northern Securities Company.

In all, Roosevelt brought 43 lawsuits against large corporations. He also created the Bureau of Corporations to report on businesses. For his work, Roosevelt became known as the Trust Buster.

Roosevelt continued to help workers, too. Coal miners had unsafe jobs. Sometimes they were injured in the mines. And, they had to work more than 12 hours every day!

So in 1902, coal miners went on strike. Roosevelt helped their unions talk to the mine owners. The two groups were able to reach an agreement. Then, Roosevelt created the Department of Commerce and Labor. This organization helped American workers receive fair treatment. Roosevelt called his policies a Square Deal.

SUPREME COURT APPOINTMENTS

OLIVER WENDELL HOLMES JR. - 1902
WILLIAM R. DAY - 1903
WILLIAM H. MOODY - 1906

During this time, ships had to sail long distances to get from the Atlantic Ocean to the Pacific Ocean. They had to go all the way around South America! Roosevelt passed laws to get a canal built through present-day Panama. The Panama Canal made travel faster for ships. This made it easier for countries to trade with each other.

President Roosevelt rode in a steam shovel to inspect the canal construction.

A Second Term

In 1904, **Republicans** nominated Roosevelt for president. His **running mate** was Indiana senator Charles Fairbanks. New York lawyer Alton Parker was the **Democratic** nominee. Henry Davis of West Virginia was his running mate.

On November 8, Roosevelt defeated Parker by 2.5 million votes. It was the greatest popular victory in history. Roosevelt was **inaugurated** on March 4, 1905.

That year, Russia and Japan were fighting the **Russo-Japanese War**. President Roosevelt met with Russian and Japanese leaders. He helped them work out their disagreements. On September 5, they signed the Treaty of Portsmouth. In 1906, Roosevelt won the **Nobel Peace Prize** for his efforts.

Left to right: *Sergi Witte and Roman Rosen of Russia, President Roosevelt, and Komura Jutaro and Takahira Kogoro of Japan signed the Treaty of Portsmouth.*

President Roosevelt's Cabinet

FIRST TERM
September 14, 1901– March 4, 1905

- **STATE –** John Hay
- **TREASURY –** Lyman J. Gage
  Leslie M. Shaw (from February 1, 1902)
- **WAR –** Elihu Root
  William Taft (from February 1, 1904)
- **NAVY –** John D. Long
  William Moody (from May 1, 1902)
  Paul Morton (from July 1, 1904)
- **ATTORNEY GENERAL –** Philander C. Knox
  William Moody (from July 1, 1904)
- **INTERIOR –** Ethan A. Hitchcock
- **AGRICULTURE –** James Wilson
- **COMMERCE AND LABOR –**
  George B. Cortelyou (from February 16, 1903)
  Victor H. Metcalf (from July 1, 1904)

SECOND TERM
March 4, 1905– March 4, 1909

- **STATE –** John Hay
  Elihu Root (from July 19, 1905)
  Robert Bacon (from January 27, 1909)
- **TREASURY –** Leslie M. Shaw
  George B. Cortelyou (from March 4, 1907)
- **WAR –** William Taft
  Luke E. Wright (from July 1, 1908)
- **NAVY –** Paul Morton
  Charles J. Bonaparte (from July 1, 1905)
  Victor H. Metcalf (from December 17, 1906)
  Truman H. Newberry (from December 1, 1908)
- **ATTORNEY GENERAL –** William Moody
  Charles J. Bonaparte (from December 17, 1906)
- **INTERIOR –** Ethan A. Hitchcock
  James R. Garfield (from March 4, 1907)
- **AGRICULTURE –** James Wilson
- **COMMERCE AND LABOR –** Victor H. Metcalf
  Oscar S. Straus (from December 17, 1906)

Roosevelt still loved **natural history** and being outdoors. He wanted to preserve land for the future. So in 1906, he signed the **Antiquities Act**.

Roosevelt also created five national parks, 18 national monuments, and 51 wildlife refuges. To manage public lands, he created the U.S. Forest Service. In all, Roosevelt preserved 230 million acres (93 million ha) of land.

Roosevelt declared the Grand Canyon a national monument on January 11, 1908.

Roosevelt also continued to work for reform. In 1906, he signed the Pure Food and Drug Act. This law helped consumers determine if foods were safe. That same year, Roosevelt signed the Meat Inspection Act. It forced meat packers to make sure the meat they sold was safe to eat.

At the end of his term, Roosevelt did not want to run for reelection. In 1908, he supported **Secretary of War** William Taft for president. Taft won the election, and Roosevelt left the White House for new adventures.

Taft (right) did not really want to be president. He wanted to serve on the U.S. Supreme Court. After his presidency he got his wish. President Warren G. Harding named him to the Court in 1921.

BULL MOOSE ADVENTURER

In March 1909, Roosevelt went to Africa to hunt big game. He killed more than 500 animals and birds. Then, he donated them for use in scientific research. Many were sent to the Smithsonian Institution in Washington, D.C.

Back in the United States, Roosevelt decided to run for president again. This time, he ran in a new political party. It was called the **Progressive** Party. It became known as the Bull Moose Party. This was because Roosevelt said he felt as strong as a bull moose!

There were three presidential candidates in the 1912 election. President Taft and Vice President James S. Sherman were the **Republican** candidates. The **Democrats** chose New Jersey governor Woodrow Wilson and Indiana governor Thomas Marshall. Roosevelt ran with California governor Hiram Johnson for the Progressive Party. Wilson won the election.

In January 1914, Roosevelt had his last big adventure. He traveled to Brazil. He hiked through jungles and sailed down rivers. Roosevelt fell from his boat, cut his leg, and he became ill.

Roosevelt never fully regained his health. By 1918, he was blind in his left eye. He also could not hear out of his left ear. On January 6, 1919, Theodore Roosevelt died in his sleep at Sagamore Hill. He was 60 years old.

Roosevelt worked hard against **corruption**. He passed laws to help workers. He went to war when he felt it necessary. But, he also worked to end war. Thanks to Roosevelt, Americans enjoy millions of acres of unspoiled land. People around the world will benefit from Theodore Roosevelt's work far into the future.

Roosevelt on the campaign trail as a Bull Moose candidate

OFFICE OF THE PRESIDENT

BRANCHES OF GOVERNMENT

The U.S. government is divided into three branches. They are the executive, legislative, and judicial branches. This division is called a separation of powers. Each branch has some power over the others. This is called a system of checks and balances.

EXECUTIVE BRANCH

The executive branch enforces laws. It is made up of the president, the vice president, and the president's cabinet. The president represents the United States around the world. He or she oversees relations with other countries and signs treaties. The president signs bills into law and appoints officials and federal judges. He or she also leads the military and manages government workers.

LEGISLATIVE BRANCH

The legislative branch makes laws, maintains the military, and regulates trade. It also has the power to declare war. This branch consists of the Senate and the House of Representatives. Together, these two houses make up Congress. Each state has two senators. A state's population determines the number of representatives it has.

JUDICIAL BRANCH

The judicial branch interprets laws. It consists of district courts, courts of appeals, and the Supreme Court. District courts try cases. If a person disagrees with a trial's outcome, he or she may appeal. If the courts of appeals support the ruling, a person may appeal to the Supreme Court. The Supreme Court also makes sure that laws follow the U.S. Constitution.

QUALIFICATIONS FOR OFFICE

To be president, a person must meet three requirements. A candidate must be at least 35 years old and a natural-born U.S. citizen. He or she must also have lived in the United States for at least 14 years.

ELECTORAL COLLEGE

The U.S. presidential election is an indirect election. Voters from each state choose electors to represent them in the Electoral College. The number of electors from each state is based on population. Each elector has one electoral vote. Electors are pledged to cast their vote for the candidate who receives the highest number of popular votes in their state. A candidate must receive the majority of Electoral College votes to win.

TERM OF OFFICE

Each president may be elected to two four-year terms. Sometimes, a president may only be elected once. This happens if he or she served more than two years of the previous president's term.

The presidential election is held on the Tuesday after the first Monday in November. The president is sworn in on January 20 of the following year. At that time, he or she takes the oath of office:

I do solemnly swear (or affirm) that I will faithfully execute the office of President of the United States, and will to the best of my ability, preserve, protect and defend the Constitution of the United States.

LINE OF SUCCESSION

The Presidential Succession Act of 1947 defines who becomes president if the president cannot serve. The vice president is first in the line of succession. Next are the Speaker of the House and the President Pro Tempore of the Senate. If none of these individuals is able to serve, the office falls to the president's cabinet members. They would take office in the order in which each department was created:

Secretary of State

Secretary of the Treasury

Secretary of Defense

Attorney General

Secretary of the Interior

Secretary of Agriculture

Secretary of Commerce

Secretary of Labor

Secretary of Health and Human Services

Secretary of Housing and Urban Development

Secretary of Transportation

Secretary of Energy

Secretary of Education

Secretary of Veterans Affairs

Secretary of Homeland Security

BENEFITS

- While in office, the president receives a salary of $400,000 each year. He or she lives in the White House and has 24-hour Secret Service protection.

- The president may travel on a Boeing 747 jet called Air Force One. The airplane can accommodate 70 passengers. It has kitchens, a dining room, sleeping areas, and a conference room. It also has fully equipped offices with the latest communications systems. Air Force One can fly halfway around the world before needing to refuel. It can even refuel in flight!

- If the president wishes to travel by car, he or she uses Cadillac One. Cadillac One is a Cadillac Deville. It has been modified with heavy armor and communications systems. The president takes Cadillac One along when visiting other countries if secure transportation will be needed.

- The president also travels on a helicopter called Marine One. Like the presidential car, Marine One accompanies the president when traveling abroad if necessary.

- Sometimes, the president needs to get away and relax with family and friends. Camp David is the official presidential retreat. It is located in the cool, wooded mountains in Maryland. The U.S. Navy maintains the retreat, and the U.S. Marine Corps keeps it secure. The camp offers swimming, tennis, golf, and hiking.

- When the president leaves office, he or she receives Secret Service protection for ten more years. He or she also receives a yearly pension of $191,300 and funding for office space, supplies, and staff.

PRESIDENTS AND THEIR TERMS

PRESIDENT	PARTY	TOOK OFFICE	LEFT OFFICE	TERMS SERVED	VICE PRESIDENT
George Washington	None	April 30, 1789	March 4, 1797	Two	John Adams
John Adams	Federalist	March 4, 1797	March 4, 1801	One	Thomas Jefferson
Thomas Jefferson	Democratic-Republican	March 4, 1801	March 4, 1809	Two	Aaron Burr, George Clinton
James Madison	Democratic-Republican	March 4, 1809	March 4, 1817	Two	George Clinton, Elbridge Gerry
James Monroe	Democratic-Republican	March 4, 1817	March 4, 1825	Two	Daniel D. Tompkins
John Quincy Adams	Democratic-Republican	March 4, 1825	March 4, 1829	One	John C. Calhoun
Andrew Jackson	Democrat	March 4, 1829	March 4, 1837	Two	John C. Calhoun, Martin Van Buren
Martin Van Buren	Democrat	March 4, 1837	March 4, 1841	One	Richard M. Johnson
William H. Harrison	Whig	March 4, 1841	April 4, 1841	Died During First Term	John Tyler
John Tyler	Whig	April 6, 1841	March 4, 1845	Completed Harrison's Term	Office Vacant
James K. Polk	Democrat	March 4, 1845	March 4, 1849	One	George M. Dallas
Zachary Taylor	Whig	March 5, 1849	July 9, 1850	Died During First Term	Millard Fillmore

34

PRESIDENT	PARTY	TOOK OFFICE	LEFT OFFICE	TERMS SERVED	VICE PRESIDENT
Millard Fillmore	Whig	July 10, 1850	March 4, 1853	Completed Taylor's Term	Office Vacant
Franklin Pierce	Democrat	March 4, 1853	March 4, 1857	One	William R.D. King
James Buchanan	Democrat	March 4, 1857	March 4, 1861	One	John C. Breckinridge
Abraham Lincoln	Republican	March 4, 1861	April 15, 1865	Served One Term, Died During Second Term	Hannibal Hamlin, Andrew Johnson
Andrew Johnson	Democrat	April 15, 1865	March 4, 1869	Completed Lincoln's Second Term	Office Vacant
Ulysses S. Grant	Republican	March 4, 1869	March 4, 1877	Two	Schuyler Colfax, Henry Wilson
Rutherford B. Hayes	Republican	March 3, 1877	March 4, 1881	One	William A. Wheeler
James A. Garfield	Republican	March 4, 1881	September 19, 1881	Died During First Term	Chester Arthur
Chester Arthur	Republican	September 20, 1881	March 4, 1885	Completed Garfield's Term	Office Vacant
Grover Cleveland	Democrat	March 4, 1885	March 4, 1889	One	Thomas A. Hendricks
Benjamin Harrison	Republican	March 4, 1889	March 4, 1893	One	Levi P. Morton
Grover Cleveland	Democrat	March 4, 1893	March 4, 1897	One	Adlai E. Stevenson
William McKinley	Republican	March 4, 1897	September 14, 1901	Served One Term, Died During Second Term	Garret A. Hobart, Theodore Roosevelt

PRESIDENT	PARTY	TOOK OFFICE	LEFT OFFICE	TERMS SERVED	VICE PRESIDENT
Theodore Roosevelt	Republican	September 14, 1901	March 4, 1909	Completed McKinley's Second Term, Served One Term	Office Vacant, Charles Fairbanks
William Taft	Republican	March 4, 1909	March 4, 1913	One	James S. Sherman
Woodrow Wilson	Democrat	March 4, 1913	March 4, 1921	Two	Thomas R. Marshall
Warren G. Harding	Republican	March 4, 1921	August 2, 1923	Died During First Term	Calvin Coolidge
Calvin Coolidge	Republican	August 3, 1923	March 4, 1929	Completed Harding's Term, Served One Term	Office Vacant, Charles Dawes
Herbert Hoover	Republican	March 4, 1929	March 4, 1933	One	Charles Curtis
Franklin D. Roosevelt	Democrat	March 4, 1933	April 12, 1945	Served Three Terms, Died During Fourth Term	John Nance Garner, Henry A. Wallace, Harry S. Truman
Harry S. Truman	Democrat	April 12, 1945	January 20, 1953	Completed Roosevelt's Fourth Term, Served One Term	Office Vacant, Alben Barkley
Dwight D. Eisenhower	Republican	January 20, 1953	January 20, 1961	Two	Richard Nixon
John F. Kennedy	Democrat	January 20, 1961	November 22, 1963	Died During First Term	Lyndon B. Johnson
Lyndon B. Johnson	Democrat	November 22, 1963	January 20, 1969	Completed Kennedy's Term, Served One Term	Office Vacant, Hubert H. Humphrey
Richard Nixon	Republican	January 20, 1969	August 9, 1974	Completed First Term, Resigned During Second Term	Spiro T. Agnew, Gerald Ford

PRESIDENT	PARTY	TOOK OFFICE	LEFT OFFICE	TERMS SERVED	VICE PRESIDENT
Gerald Ford	Republican	August 9, 1974	January 20, 1977	Completed Nixon's Second Term	Nelson A. Rockefeller
Jimmy Carter	Democrat	January 20, 1977	January 20, 1981	One	Walter Mondale
Ronald Reagan	Republican	January 20, 1981	January 20, 1989	Two	George H.W. Bush
George H.W. Bush	Republican	January 20, 1989	January 20, 1993	One	Dan Quayle
Bill Clinton	Democrat	January 20, 1993	January 20, 2001	Two	Al Gore
George W. Bush	Republican	January 20, 2001	January 20, 2009	Two	Dick Cheney
Barack Obama	Democrat	January 20, 2009			Joe Biden

"The conservation of natural resources is the fundamental problem. Unless we solve that problem it will avail us little to solve all others." Theodore Roosevelt

WRITE TO THE PRESIDENT

You may write to the president at:

**The White House
1600 Pennsylvania Avenue NW
Washington, DC 20500**

You may e-mail the president at:

comments@whitehouse.gov

GLOSSARY

Antiquities Act - a law passed in 1906. It gives the U.S. president authority to preserve landmarks, structures, and other objects of historic or scientific interest that are located on land owned or controlled by the U.S. government.

assassin - someone who murders a very important person, usually for political reasons.

asthma - a condition that causes wheezing and coughing and makes breathing difficult.

civil service - the part of the government that is responsible for matters not covered by the military, the courts, or the law.

corruption - dishonest or improper behavior.

Democrat - a member of the Democratic political party. When Theodore Roosevelt was president, Democrats supported farmers and landowners.

discrimination (dihs-krih-muh-NAY-shuhn) - unfair treatment based on factors such as a person's race, religion, or gender.

inaugurate (ih-NAW-gyuh-rayt) - to swear into a political office.

lawsuit - a case held before a court.

natural history - the study of objects found in nature, such as animals, plants, and minerals.

Nobel Peace Prize - a prize given each year to a person who works hard for world peace.

Progressive - a member of one of several Progressive political parties organized in the United States. Progressives believed in liberal social, political, and economic reform.

Republican - a member of the Republican political party. When Theodore Roosevelt was president, Republicans supported business and strong government.

running mate - a candidate running for a lower-rank position on an election ticket, especially the candidate for vice president.

Russo-Japanese War - from 1904 to 1905. A war between Russia and Japan. They fought for control of Korea and Manchuria.

secretary of the navy - a member of the president's cabinet who heads the Department of the Navy.

secretary of war - a member of the president's cabinet who handles the nation's defense.

Spanish-American War - a war between the United States and Spain in 1898. At the end of the war, Spain freed Cuba and signed over Guam, the Philippines, and Puerto Rico to the United States.

spoils system - a practice of giving people jobs or taking away jobs because of political beliefs.

trust - a group of companies joined by a legal agreement, which stops competition over a good or a service.

tutor - someone who teaches a student privately.

WEB SITES

To learn more about Theodore Roosevelt, visit ABDO Publishing Company on the World Wide Web at **www.abdopublishing.com**. Web sites about Theodore Roosevelt are featured on our Book Links page. These links are routinely monitored and updated to provide the most current information available.

INDEX